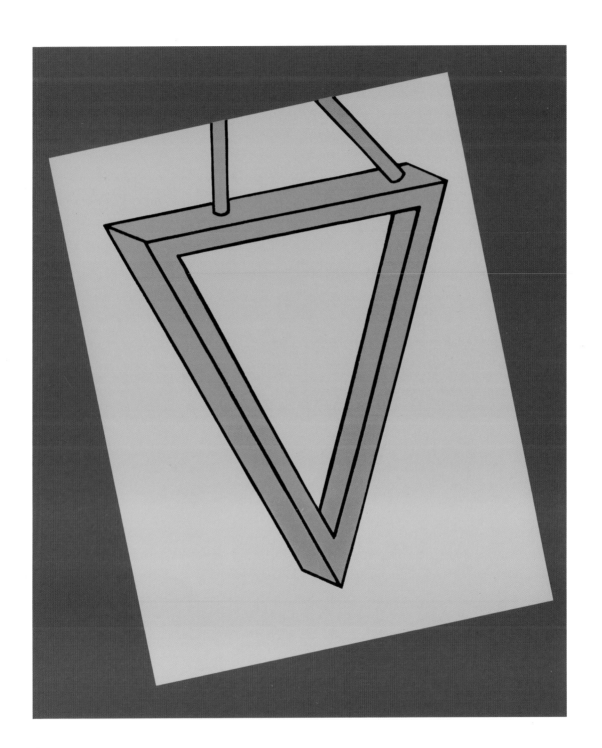

CYBERSPACE

CYBERSPACE

KENWARD ELMSLIE

&

TREVOR WINKFIELD

GRANARY BOOKS   NEW YORK CITY   2000

Acknowledgement is made to the following publications in which
sections of the poem, sometimes in variant versions, appeared:
Faucheuse: "Diddly Squat"
Neotrope: "Solo Imbroglio, Bub Irruptions"

ISBN 1-887123-33-4

Book design by Julie Harrison & Trevor Winkfield
The types are Stempel Garamond and Trajan

Printed (on acid-free paper) and bound in Hong Kong April, 2000

The edition is limited to 3,000 copies in wrappers
of which 26 are lettered and signed by the poet and artist

Granary Books, Inc.
307 Seventh Ave., #1401
New York, NY 10001

www.granarybooks.com
info@granarybooks.com

Distributed by:
D.A.P. (Distributed Art Publishers)
155 Ave. of the Americas
New York, NY 10013
&
Small Press Distribution
1341 Seventh Street
Berkeley, CA 94710

For

William Cohen

&

C W

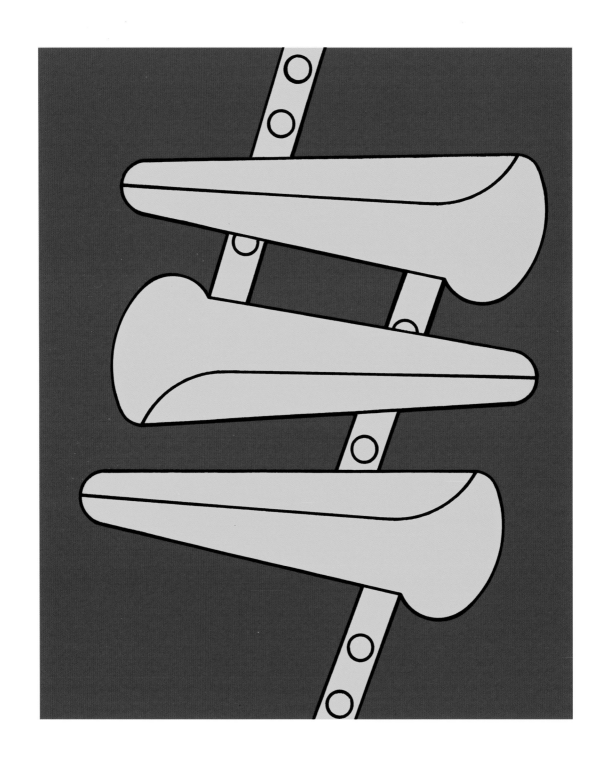

I. ROCK BOTTOM

MOTOR MOUTHS, GRANTED, but hey, I've come to enjoy overflow. Key
meltdown of frou-frou festoons defiled my website's swelter-
ing (still uninhabited because uninhabitable) sacred loci.
Detoxed, total recall's a rarity, but last vernal equinox, I felt a

swale of pathos re a veldt epiphany, hula hoop imbedded in dung, ho-
ho cartoon an e-biz logo. Clip art lip line of marsupial pouch gappy.
Peering out, saucer-eyed whelp — turquoise 'roo. Gung-ho
promo to hurl on the pyre, should my blood orange futures co-opt me: slaphappy

new lifestyle, ha-ha, surfeit of Netscape wake-up calls in impenetrable tech argot.
"Hot sex, a sniff job … still warm tricycle seat of Delia the Moppet quadroon.
Share a Snickers, dearie?" Dreamt. Say I say that on a tram in Alabam', at, heck, Fargo
& Pell St. — that swell street … *I be downsized ghats of Hell* … sad rune.

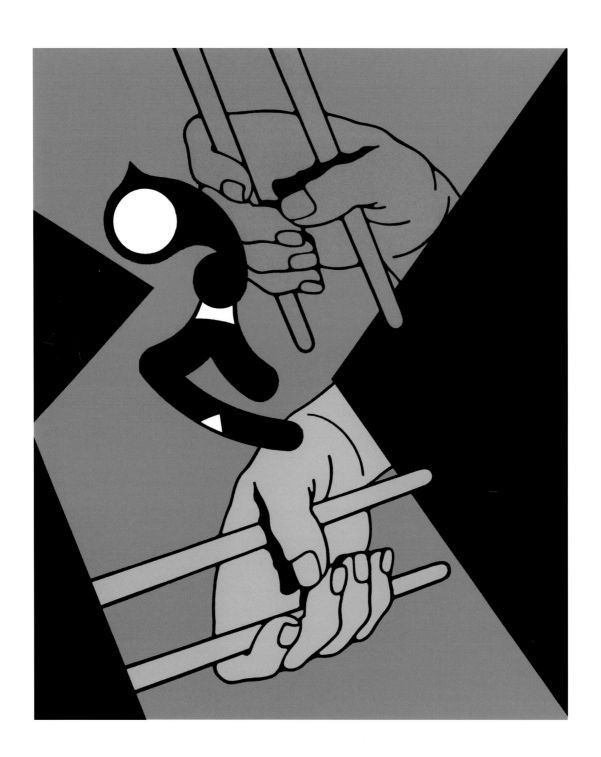

Back to overflow. The cremation instructions are behind a loose brick
behind a loose cannon. Sit ye doon, Sri and Lady Jessup. He
is in Parsi lanyards, she dotted Swiss nipple nappies for prick-
heads like you, Queen Beef Curtain. Oh, no! In flames! The coronation recipe!

To resuscitate the muss, braise and dust. Can Do, but regurgitated posse gunk …
dusk, stark terror'll kick in. Antarctica. The lunar Urals. Patagonia. Sssh!
Dusk just fell. Must host a slamdunk of lunar buzz words, why, clunk clunk,
(iffy consensus) siroccos swish by with lugubrious aplomb. "Thelonius!

Come in the pod this sec and watch Daddy e-mail Al Nussbaum" — a
name he, I think he's a he, goes by, though his chat room alias is *Tim's*, um,
Dildo. Al does dawn of history restructurings. Averts die-down trauma.
Prescient which way the beige charts'll veer. Hey! Shall we polish off the dim sum?

Jibber-jabber about my new browser, ground-level know-how, her groupie *thang*. Sod babe exclusivity. Pick up Nazi Nite Smile muff, white angora bobbysox. Neo-puppylove Retro-30s.

Can Do Savant sugarcoats our pillow gab.
Match, Bub? In Iwo Gig foxhole simulate
same-sex frottage. Guffaws signal viruses
infest throughput. Scarf uranium formula
as four redneck doughboys duke it out. A

molten mass cascades through Times Sq.
His *Cut it out, Bub* is so accusatory, I try
to incriminate him. He demeans my lack
charisma. Revenge! Hall-of-Mirrors flak
unmasks him: recidivist Virgin Schtupper.

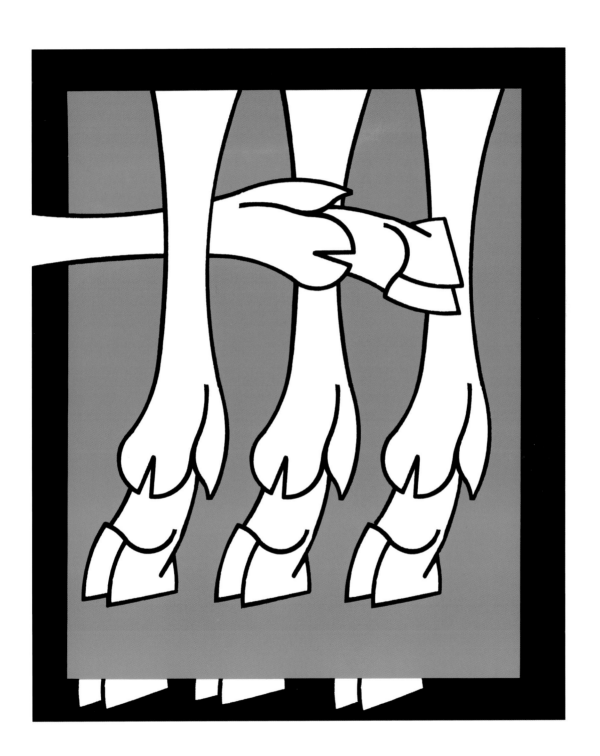

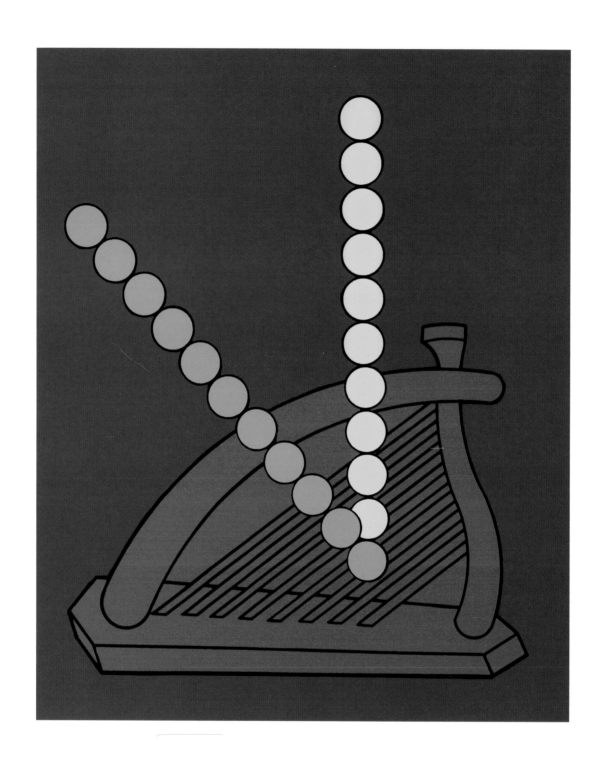

Last spring, didn't nail clippers drive fuddy-duddy dolly toes batty?
Wish List: Peace in our luncheonette. More egalitarian kickbacks.
No frantic beeps from dysfunctional hand-helds to hype repro *Hulots* (Tati).
Sign up time. I salud Jacques, my maimed hero bro. Mami-bound (sic). *Pax*!

Enough scabrous adventurism. Zephyrs stress their own support systems
of devotional tiles, stilts and eddies. Hear 'em snuffle and sputter?
But that's no reason to give up! Installations shimmer so in mist, Thames
befogged. I'm bushed, granted, but if Londonton ever implodes, gutter-

snipe street smarts'll coarsen and traduce control freak frigidities. Dethroned,
psycho ward case histories of scant archival interest to my veggie regimen.
Mustn't forget spray fixatives on burgeoning folder (U) Citizen A-1 phoned
in. Mustn't scroll *Unearned Intimacy* (sea chantey) or anti-Red edgy G-Men

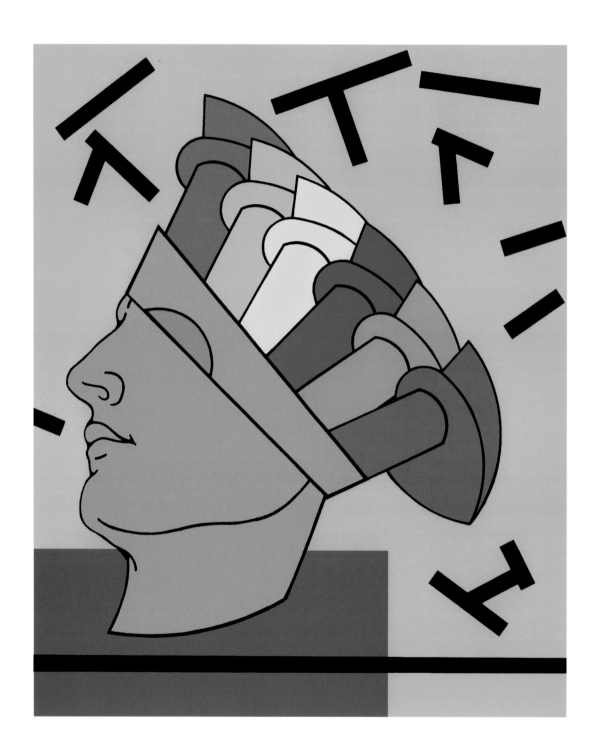

'll be emasculated. Down to cases. What I do best? Excoriate and floogle suck the corpus.
Stripped, it invalidates hereafter chutzpah. At midnight, tottery stiffs,
marginal disposables, line up for the quorum on the gurney, porpoise
rictus implanted. Makes fatal illness user-friendlier. I love it when whiffs

of eternal rest aroma therapy kick in and whammed cadavers regain gut pulse.
In mid-maelstrom came the fax — *earnings anomalies plague liquids.*
Apocalyptic fizz? E-Bay's dotty Custer's Last Stand qualms are what? Cults?
Sky war survivors of black geysers. Origin — an effluvia tic (squids).

That happens, habit kicked, deserted wharf, skirt caught in locked steamer trunk.
Future joblessness, meatlessness. Stinko, Bub and I missed the last bus.
Hoofed it. Why reinvent the wheel online via an all-pixel dream? Grrrr! Drunk,
we smashed the *NextPreviousHome* server that'd so relentlessly harassed us.

II. SOLO IMBROGLIO

SAVE ME FROM SOLO IMBROGLIO my new credo. Maniacal gurgle just my stomach's,
from *Tofu Banane*, brandied pomegranates topping. Power brunch with hot site consultant.
Royal rush. Burnt out by gigabit mirroring is my guess. Behaved like a lummox.
Crouch, unzip, nice butt. Outa there — suspect childhood trauma: doomsday cult. Aunt

Tabitha so like her, ego a black hole. Interactive voice response, ergo, has too thin a veil.
Ergo, shelf-life bottlenecks. Ergo, warehousing in remote sites goes unmonitored.
One Badlands Halloween, host platform backup demolished bank-at-home firewalls. Holy Grail
mainframe zealots raided Tulsa: Easter disaster. Xmas '98, data center shat out a bonny turd.

Funny money decal coins gummed up tax haven jackpots. Offshore, bubble-wrapped,
Auntie T wound up in a bruise-free Isle of Man nut-house. "Keep me safe from downtime,
Help Desk! Over to you, Help Desk! Help Desk? Get me Help Desk!" Double strapped,
jaw jutting, nose hole cones unswabbed, she'd shriek (from *On The Town*) "I'm

So Lucky To Be …" Pause. Donald Duck mimicry. *Screamy Me* her last mantra.
She willed me her epaulettes and shako (Lotus Award, storage capacity containment),
and her ivory silk IBM cummerbund, blood-stained (conspiracy theory charisma). You *can* tra-
ditionalize honorifics, even if wait-listed for a unisex nirvana. Her narrative-driven brain meant

to movie-musicalize her vita. Left me a triple-mirror screen treatment. Sea-plane lifts off for Rio.
Credits (Irene Dunne) roll as the ice-floes (Bob Hope) that keep her archipelago
pre-pill, pre-*Wozzeck*, pre-Mickey Rooney (Mickey Rooney), pre-sanitary napkins, pre-B.O.
(body odor, not Box Office) dissolve. *J'accuse*! B.O. Suit & Tie Fridays make a fella go

bimbo. Exec washroom key? Hush money? Shove it! All too soon I became poopdeck uppity.
Then Y2K loopholes made their move. My wife got custody, pink Cad drawn by rickety nag.
I clambered on it. Mist. Roseate dust particles hosed off by *un vrai* educational Muppet. He
had googly-googly eyes, handed me "Your Diamond Horseshoe ducat, Bub." My first e-gag.

Our first cigarillo a come-on. He goes for boozy nape breath. *Cut it out, Bub!* a gob sex come-on so natshurly I went He-She. Fun clientele kinky. Suffered flashbacks, name's Glabys Hitler, bunk with Eva, Rooshians. Lighten up, Dolfy. I do my laffgetter. "Ever page-turn *Under The Bleachers* by Seymour Butt?" Silence. Just bombs bursting.

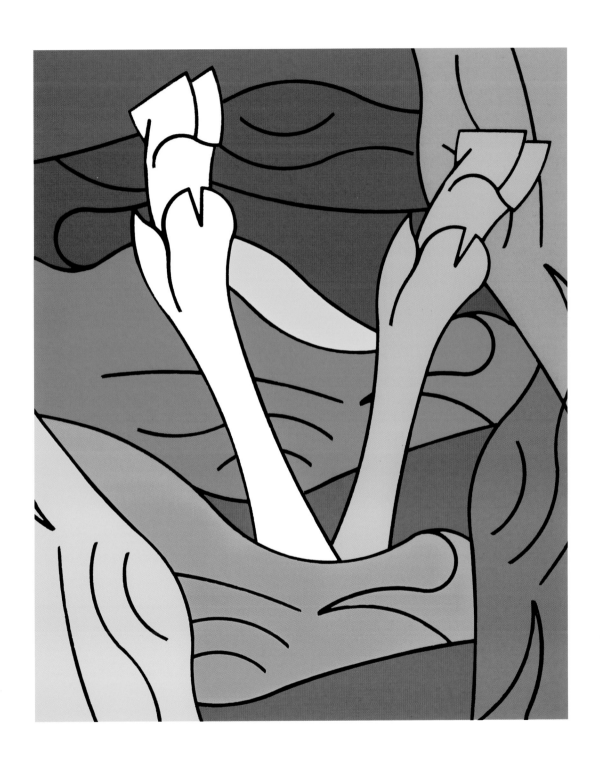

Guess what? Thirty flirty years later, look us up inner city. We do Chicken Mambo Scenectiddy.

Mon-Sat Jambalaya extry fiery for ethnic rice queens with catalyst: coolsig menu capability.

Bubba & Muffy's www.BBQ.com. Ultra-sound on fleecy cloudbanks a la Frozi & Gigi. You earthlings & swingle heads love speed short haul cycle! Dial up docuprint but pulleez! No queer screenlessness!

Wearing my purple terry stare out past sliding glass at Tribune tower. Nite Flash!
B-U-B-H-O-M-E-T-O-W-N-S-O-L-D-F-O-R-T-O-R-N-A-D-O-M-O-V-I-E!
Icebox gone zinnias my matchwrapper Elvis Ringo mood ring … po' white trash
bungalow. Sign: Sis Dorene's Witness Protection Ski Masks 1/2 Price Groovy,

one window. Orange hula-hula girlie lamp, plum hips wobble, when lit turn pear,
other window, plus unsent Jesus Fountain ad, red freshets gushing from his stigmata.
Gone, the crank-it-up Victrola, back when golden hunks sang, betuxed, debonair,
of Easy Street glut, back alley lust. Me and Dorene, in her hoi polloi mahatma shmatta,

we'd zigzag up Alamo Boulevard's hairpin curves, over Pig Snout Pass
to hard scrabble flatland, paranoid blues centrum of hipster mannequins. Blip.
Time to take control. Gobble high bandwidth and ad hoc access to gigabit crevasse.
Why fleece the enemy within? Reassess workflow, little things like panic kinship.

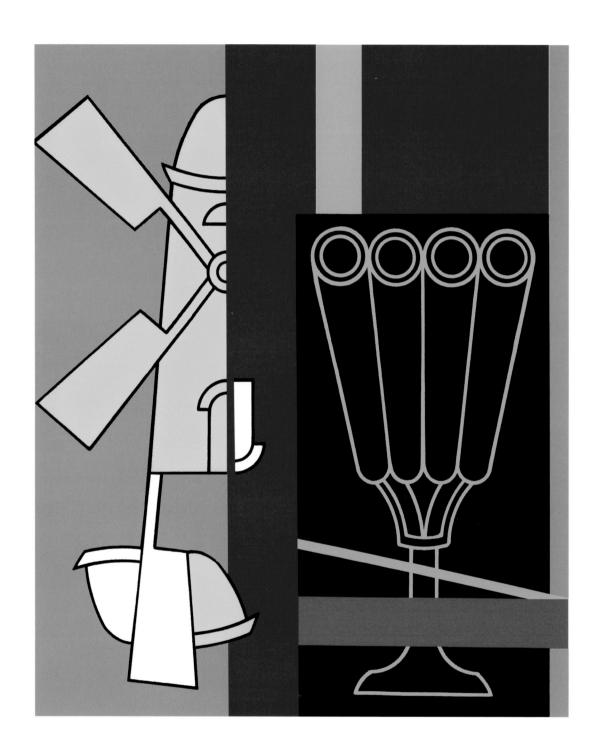

More overflow, in hosp. Dad's AWOL, not a nickel to his name.
Jailhouse Mum bush-hogged his pork-pie hat, ten years ago. Brag, brag. Balloon
above Davy Crockett's Mall whupped by the wind. Smells kinda nice, K-Mart aflame.
Babe, need a spree in paradise, pine to fricassee that ol' scumbag moon.

No picnic, wedding of John Barry Ryan IV and Dorinda "Tennis Elbow" McCloud.
Soused to the gills, my outer mask held firm. Terrible year. Climacteric?
Short-term memory loss. Glossolalia. Mood, black. Vowed
to control my miasma of quasi-narcissism. Trapped in a sitcom, me, sublime actor. Ick.

You impersonate my identical twin. Bio overload. Bird-brained idiosyncrasies.
Pushover for Retro Chic: strip poker with the youth spook in the gazebo. You stall,
raffishly bundled up, Tam o' Shanter, hush puppies video pink. You sneeze.
I order you to "batten down the hatches." Underfoot, pine needles crunch. It's fall.

III.   DIDDLY SQUAT

POLLY VU CAMCORD, incandescent. 9:03, #1 Hot Prod, my *Shibboleth for a Welterweight*.
9:04, Dorene's *Lady Burford Unveiled*, gamelan pings and outsource hubbub irresistable.
Mood swings, vast improvement. My lesbian HMO therapist has lasered LOVE-HATE
off my knuckles, reward for wet dream recall: Clark Gable. Me kiss his stubble,

post-coital, despite his awful mustache and dead meat smell. Buggered asprawl my teepee.
Hollywood beckons. Sahara Arab-Ute boy, me, oasis pastorale, me, abandoned! GWTW Rhett.
Update. Rebirth *joie de vivre* ebulliant. Hold up right hand, home room, permission pee-pee.
Hayloft. Sausage curls, squat. Warm girl, wet on my fingers. Deep trouble? You bet!

Began my mystic selfhood struggle, wended my way past youth fetish dichotomies.
Update. On screen: bald men, weekly pinochle, watch screen. Drops, *e-prix* of macadamia crop
they've bet the ranch on. The interstices, that's the crux. Get cracking, Bozo. The sleaze
factor, e-porn to micro-manage. Fag hags flouncing about in chinchilla maim me atop —

9:05, *Whisper Money*, Aunt Tabitha's elegaic farrago mustn't be overlooked.
Jagged mountains see-saw as, at the schooner's wheel, she eats a banana.
Flashback. Berates the serving laddy. Corn-on-the-cob mustn't be overcooked.
Flash forward. Mafioso folds century in her cleavage. Havana.

"I'm Reuben The Cuban" — ballistic half-bro slips into the surf, unannounced.
Random January. An ingenious smegma-of-an-ant roadmap led me there.
Wiped off my tears, oil rag. Argument about pine barren for Aryans. Pounced
on Ida, motel maze. Picnic leftovers Saran-wrapped in fridge gave me a Dead Me Scare.

Furry growths, deep sea stillness. 9:06: *Asleep At The Switch*. Me up at bat again,
talky oldie. Twin beds, shadows kiss. Prudes were in the saddle, Marxist regime.
Defensive, me? Request. Please don't sing "Does anyone still wear a hat?" again.
Alone, same old bitch on wheels, a-sea, hypnotized by a shark's cyst. E-dream:

dinner with Ron and Pat, sense of continuity feathery tail sweeps up. Deep marijuana nap. *Aluminum siding* is nightmare bar highpoint. Wild-repressed Irish slovenliness. Rip rushes about, Kenward won't speak to me Kenward won't speak to me. Suicide threat, taxi to his loft. Speed speed speed. Everything so small and boring. Drift from one day next. A speed vegetable now. Barely recognizable fragment of former self. Starts touching me which I resist firmly. His project *The Red Book*. He can move into the top floor, I tell him. Easier give up speed in a different environment. No fucky and not living with me, two problems I resent.

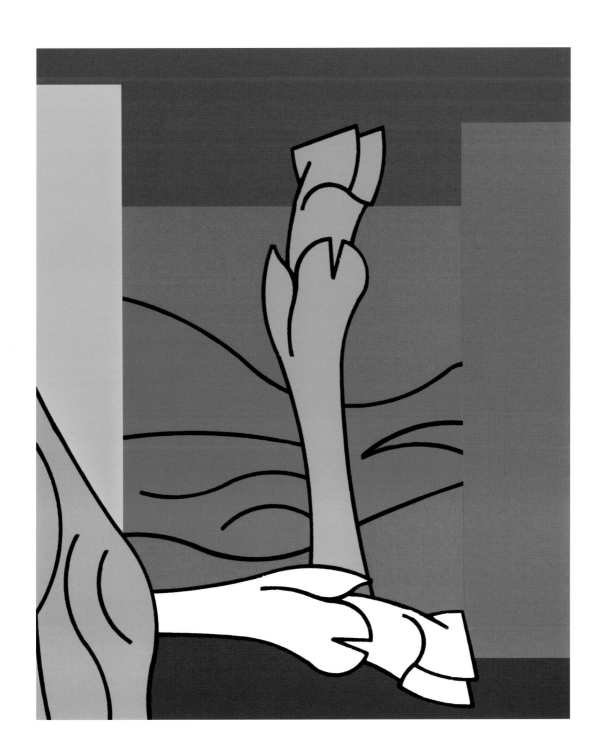

sorry not more daring jaywalk calm day job objectivity unhinged by his cringe posture. Punish me for ghost voice's interminable churring. He's forgotten who he came for … kitchen

— raid icebox. Banana peel in sink, credit card's back in its regular spot (must venture out more). Do upscale

spas and memory jogs, with spherical outgo containers, so U don't ever need slog to the P.O. in the slush. C U (*)

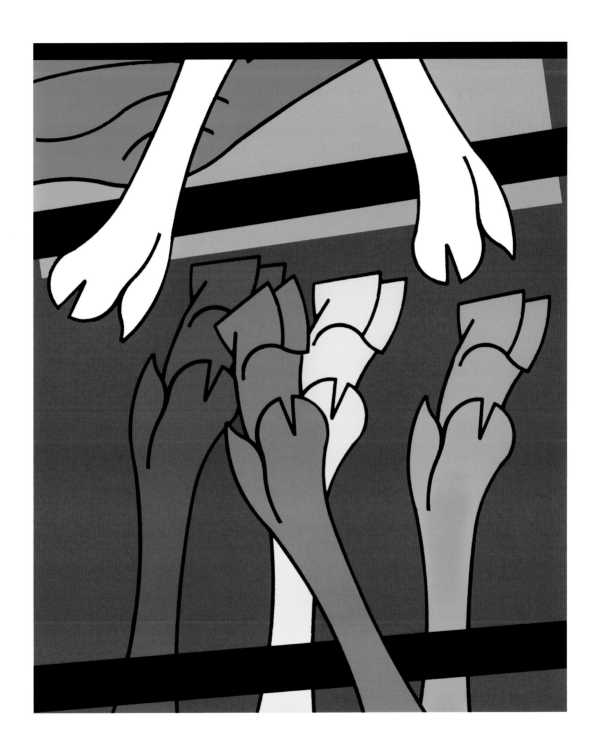

Motor mouth overflow has tapered off. I head home. Dish with CW how Wayne's a wife-beater.
Carlos asks Ruth for a blow job. She tells him direct approach a turn-off. Prefers Romance.
Derek has white-streaked hair now, looks old. In Paris, we ordered *vin ordinaire* by the litre.
At the funeral, his step-bro Chuck spreads the word, Derek has ants in his asshole pants.

I move to a new megalopolis. Hyperactive flower child asks me, "Who's *your* guru, Bozo?"
Obligatory Q & A, pro or con *Marrow Gobs*, imposter-surgeon infrastructure skinflick.
Same day, impromptu wave to Al on funicular to the morgue. He struck raffish pose. So?
No dhow float for Untouchables Triathlon, fund flush toilets in sister city's jinrik-

isha depots. *Jeunesse dorée* survival guilt. At two, I knew to let Sancerre breathe.
At four, special abattoir solved the foie gras conundrum. By ten, anus force-fed brains
a no-no after sunset, in labyrinthine sex warrens crumbling under the abandoned wreath
of wealth rotunda. Long since ceased and desisted live whistle-blowing. Plenty else profanes

the air I subsist on, the cocoon I curl up in to make ready for the morrow.
April, my birth month, flashed by quicker'n a chicken pursued by a musical saw robot.
After her life-affirmative mink stole punch-line, my surrogate, Missy Sorrow
'll shroud herself and prance airily up the gangplank into the showboat.

Doing OK, scouting for shards. Forgot ancestral magnifying glass under my hankies,
condoms, sox (don't always match, ribs diverge). I'm used to my bureau's muss
and I don't miss prisms unseen. Yesterday, under an assortment of dank keys,
came across a words-bunched-up epistle ending *"keepyourfilthyeuros"* plus

an unfinished PS: *"Ifyoubalanceonevernaleggina"* — signed Victor. Knock Knock,
Victor, whoever you were. In a *what*? Eidolon? *Passez-moi* some watermelon rind.
Ygg, my creation myth, still engorges Tom Courtney and his variegated ilk. Shock
of recognition has petered out. Ruts and more ruts. Hurdy-gurdy a plus, sky a find.